TROUBLE!

Illustrations and story by

Belinda Sillars

TROUBLE!

ISBN 978-1-893959-78-1

Small Paws Press
PO Box 210
Millwood VA
22646 USA

www.belindasillars.com
www.introubleagain.com

This is my true story.
I live with artist and sculptor Belinda Sillars
and 'er dogs and 'orse.

I want to thank Daisy for choosing me!

TROUBLE!

I WERE BORN!

I were bred by a family of Romanies, who were travelling through Cambridgeshire in England at the time of me birth. Me mother was a small rough-coated terrier but me father was unknown! Four of us were born. Me, I was black and white with the smallest brown splashes, and a rough coat. I 'ad short crooked legs, black ears and a very very long tail. Me bottom jaw was very very short so I never could say me aitches. Me mother said me jaw was so short due to a mishap. Someone pulling me out of an 'ole by me tail too 'ard. And as everyone knows a dog's tail is attached to its bottom jaw.

'ORSE SALE

When me family were still very small we were taken in a cardboard box to Cambridge 'orse sale. Me family were all brown and white, I was the smallest.

Lots of people came and looked at us. Finally a little girl came and picked me up, then cuddled me. She asked 'er mother if they could 'ave me, 'er mother said "yes".

I liked that.

DAISY

The little girl was called Daisy. She was small with short blond 'air and freckles all over 'er nose, and she was very pretty. She took me 'ome to meet 'er other dogs. She 'ad two terriers, Feather, who was brown and white, she 'ad really long legs, and Duster who was black and white with really short legs. I was then introduced to Flick, who was the 'ugest rottweiler you 'ave ever seen. They was all nice. This became me new family, and Daisy named me TROUBLE.

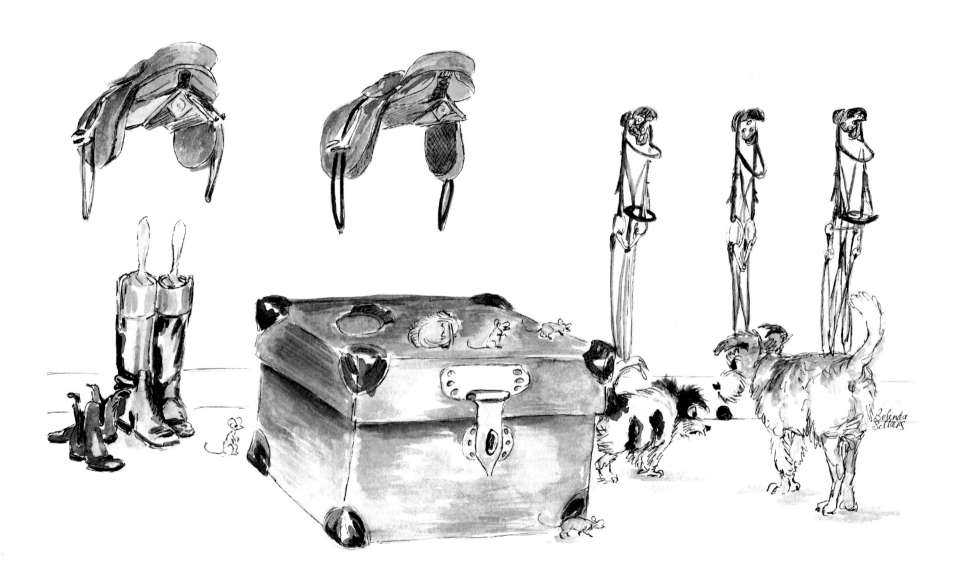

PORK PIE COUNTRY

Daisy lived in Melton Mowbury in Leicestershire, famous for its pork pies, 'ence we called it pork pie country. Lots of 'orses lived 'ere, but they didn't stay long, they always 'ad somewhere to go. Lots of comings and goings.

Flick lived outside as she was the guard dog; she took her job very seriously. Duster lived in the 'ouse and came out on a lead. Feather told me this were 'cause Duster liked to 'unt, but not at 'ome!! Feather and I lived in the stable yard, out buildings and the tack room. Flick told me to listen and learn from Feather as she was a really good 'unter. There were loads of mice around, but there were some rats in the muck 'eep.

I grew in my 'unting skills but not in size.

DUSTER

Duster could be very naughty. On these occasions she would jump out of Daisy's bedroom window. She just wanted to go 'unting. Me first time 'unting I were really excited, but me poor short crooked legs couldn't keep up with the others. I 'ad no idea where they 'ad got too. Gosh, was I 'appy when I saw Daisy come to find me, I barked with 'appiness.

A VERY BAD DAY

I is busy most days, 'unting round the yard. Daisy 'ad lots to do and I loved to follow 'er about, she would carry me a lot too.

I liked that.

I was just lazing in the sun, while Daisy was brushing one of the 'orses, when the 'orse moved over and trod on me tail. 'Is 'ooves 'ad steel shoes on, and 'e was on me tail!!!! It 'urt terrible, I did scream and scream and scream, and Daisy did scream and scream and scream.

She took me straight to the vets. I was given a 'uge injection and fell t' sleep.

When I wakes up, ME TAIL WAS GONE!!!

I was very sad. When I got 'ome Flick assured me I'd be all right in a while as she also 'ad no tail, and didn't know if she 'ad ever 'ad one or if someone 'ad stole it. Daisy and 'er friends gave me loads of cuddles; I liked all the extra attention.

BUNNY 'UNTING

Daisy was 'aving a birthday party with some of 'er friends in the garden. Naughty Duster was allowed outside but came to get us to go 'unting. Flick was tied up so couldn't come with us. We set off fast but I could keep up better now. Duster suddenly started barking. I got this funny whiff of something, it weren't mice or rats, it was also down an 'ole. BUNNIES, yippeeee. We did chase them all around and in and out of their 'oles, it was great fun.

Realizing I was getting 'ungry, I decided to find the others. Emerging from me 'ole, I discovered it was dark and the others 'ad gone. I 'ad no idea where I was. Setting off, I soon saw lights in front of me. They seemed to be moving and also making a whooshing noise. It was a road, and I was very scared. I decided to go back the way I 'ad just come. Feeling tired, so found an' ole I 'oped to sleep 'in, so I curled up tight and fell asleep. When I woke up it was light, so I tried to 'ead for 'ome. I found meself back on the road. The cars went so fast that I stayed right on the side. When a car stopped, and a lady got out, she asked me if I was lost. I wagged me stump with glee as she picked me up and put me in 'er car.

JAIL

After driving for a while the lady pulled up in front of a building. There was a lot of barking. I was 'anded over to another lady who put me in a wire pen. There were big dogs in pens next to me. I was really scared so l went to the box at the back and curled up as small as l could and tried to sleep. A bowl of food was brought for me later but l didn't dare move. l wasn't really 'ungry anymore.

I 'ave no idea 'ow long l was there. I didn't leave me box. later a kind lady came and picked me up out of me box and took me outside. I couldn't believe me eyes: there was Daisy. She did cuddle and kiss me. l was sooo 'appy. Everyone came to greet me when we got 'ome, they were so pleased to see me and l was really pleased to see them!!

NEW FRIENDS

Life went back to normal, 'unting mice and rats around the yard. People and 'orses came and went.

One morning a lady called B arrived with 'er 'orse Bramble and 'er two dogs Sprout, a short-legged, rough-coated terrier with very crooked legs, and Clemetis the most beautiful liver-spotted Dalmatian, she was so elegant.

Bramble was to stay at the yard. So B and the two dogs came twice a day to ride and look after Bramble. Sprout rode with B on Bramble and Clemetis trotted alongside, 'twas a lovely sight. We got to know them all quite well over the next few weeks. Sprout liked a bit of 'unting but Clemetis would 'ave nothing to do with it, as she didn't like letting B out of 'er sight so 'unting was difficult.

PERCY

Daisy found a racing pigeon on the drive one morning. 'e were lost. She put 'im in a box and fed 'im until 'e were strong enough to come and stay on the beams of the roof of the main stable. Feather and I thought it our job to encourage 'im to fly, so 'e could get better. Feather was tall enough to jump up on the round bales, and bark at 'im from there. I stayed on the ground and barked along with 'er. Sometimes Flick would join in from 'er chain but she just 'owled, it was quite a chorus. Percy the pigeon would just sit on 'is beam and watch us!!

THE LAST STRAW

It were an 'ot day and Daisy 'ad let Flick off 'er chain to be able to lie in the shade with us. Suddenly Duster appeared, shouting at us to 'urry up so we can go 'unting. She'd jumped out the window again, bad dog. We all raced off out the yard, Flick and Duster in the lead with Feather next and me tagging along be'ind. The fields 'ad been cut so we raced across them to the 'oles under the 'edges. What fun we 'ad running in and out. Bunnies everywhere. I barked and barked and I lost track of time. Getting thirsty I came out of an 'ole to find I was alone, I'd 'ad so much fun. But now there was no one to be seen. I wandered around trying to find some sign of anyone.

I walked and walked 'oping to find someone. I saw some farm buildings in the distance and made me way towards them. I was passing through a field of sheep when they started to stamp their feet and glare at me. They worried me so I trotted off in another direction.

I then followed the 'edge till I found a gap, which took me to a road. It wasn't too busy, so I set off 'oping I was 'eading 'ome. A car stopped and a friendly man got out. He picked me up and put me in his car. I was so tired I just went to sleep. I woke finding meself being carried into the same jail as before. OH NO!!

FRIENDS

There were nicer people next to me this time. Red on one side was a large leggy fellow. 'E 'ad been 'ere a long time. 'E 'ad been a town dog and 'ad lived all 'is life on a chain with a small shelter. 'E 'ad always been 'ungry, until 'e came 'ere, they treated 'im well and 'e was warm and fed. 'E would 'ave loved a family to call 'is own.

On me other side was Poppet who was all white and fluffy. 'Er owner was old and one morning just didn't wake up. It was sad. I tried to cheer them up with stories of bunnies and 'unting.

Some days a few people would come and look at us. It seemed I were there for days, I don't know. Suddenly I heard Daisy's voice and started barking and jumping up and down. Daisy picked me up and cuddled me. I've never been so 'appy.

NEW BEGINNINGS

Because of me 'unting 'abits I was to go and live with B, Sprout and Clemetis. B lived in a small apartment attached to a larger 'ouse. There were two other dogs living 'ere, Pongo, an old smooth-coated Jack Russell, who was shy, and Muffy, a long-legged lurcher. They were owned by Caitlin, who was a friend of Daisy's, so I knew 'er. I was really shy at first.

I saw Feather, Flick and Duster every day but didn't live with them anymore.

I were about to get me first riding lesson, I were a bit scared. I 'ad to balance on Bramble's wither, I wasn't very good, and 'ad to have an 'arness on to stop me falling off. If I did slip I would dangle down the side of Bramble's shoulder until rescued!! I tried so 'ard to concentrate, but was often thinking of bunnies, and the next I knew I was dangling again!!

We all went for a walk every day too. I was supposed to learn to come back to me name when told. I wasn't good at this either!!

Belinda Peters

TRAVELLING

We travelled a lot. B 'ad a Land Rover that was great fun. Clemetis would sit on the front passenger seat, Sprout on B's lap and I would be in between the two. As you know all Land Rovers 'ave a seat for small dogs in the middle.

Me first night away started with a long journey. Finally we turned up a long driveway. Immediately Sprout and Clemetis started barking, I 'ad no idea why but I joined in anyway. Then I saw the bunnies, they were everywhere, that's what I thought all the noise was about.

As soon as we stopped and B opened the door we all tumbled out. Me, I went 'unting. Bunnies were all over the place. I was really into it when I realized that me name was being shouted, OH OH I was in TROUBLE, BIG TROUBLE, but the bunnies were so much fun. B was cross with me for not coming when called, Oh Dear.

On me return I was introduced to Bean who was Sprout's daughter, 'er eldest. She was all white with a long tail. Bean lived with three beagles, Tilly, Squiggle and Dilly Dog. All were owned by Kim and her 'usband Nick. They were B's best friends.

Belinda Sellars

THE GREEN'OUSE

Sprout and I were 'aving a lazy day. Clemetis was in the 'ouse with B watching 'er work. Suddenly Sprout shot off toward the green'ouse and started barking at some flower pots. I 'adn't a clue what was going on but barked anyway. Sprout took a breath and shouted "MOUSE", now I knew!! Flower pots were knocked over as Sprout raced from one to t'other. I decides to go inside the green'ouse to see if I could hear the mouse from inside. YES 'e was there alright. Sprout and I started digging from opposite sides, barking all the time. Clemetis and Pongo 'ad a look but retreated to the doorstep for safety, B came out and looked and was 'orrified. All of a sudden Sprout and I were looking straight at each other. We'd dug a tunnel under the green'ouse and met in the middle! Not a mouse to be seen.

CHICKENS

After the excitement of the green'ouse, we went on a road trip. We all loved these expeditions, we 'ad such fun.

With Sprout 'elping B drive we eventually turned down a tree shaded overgrown driveway. Sprout and Clemetis wagged their tails and stood to look out the windows. I were excited too, I could see bunnies. We stopped in an old brick stableyard surrounded by large trees. We all exploded from the Land Rover and went mad chasing everything. I was suddenly brought up short, as a strange being appeared before me. It did smell odd. It 'ad longish legs and feathers and ran really fast. It 'ad sort of arm fings that it waved about. I shot after it barking as 'ard as I could, it was such fun.

Suddenly it was no longer in front of me, it 'ad flown up into a tree with all its friends, and they made more noise than me. B was shouting my name, OH OH, in TROUBLE again!!! These were chickens.

The lady that lived 'ere, Mrs Smith, 'ad three terriers. Pie was Sprout's daughter, the middle one, she was smooth-coated with brown and black patches all over. She was small like me. Pickle was mostly white with black ears and a black spot on 'is tail. Buzzie was brown and white with a rough coat. 'E was a bit of a softy, and told tales on us all the time. 'E didn't like 'unting.

Mrs Smith wasn't very 'appy with me for chasing 'er chickens, but it was soon forgotten.

THE BIG MOVE

I 'ad got used to seeing Flick, Feather and Duster, we were sometimes away for a couple of days but always came back to see Bramble and ride. I was getting much better but still needed to be more concentrated, it was so easy to be distracted!!

One day we packed everything in the Land Rover and put Bramble in the trailer, we were moving to Suffolk. This place is next door to Cambridgeshire where l were born.

Our 'ome in Suffolk was quite small, but very cozy. In the kitchen was an 'eater that we could curl up in front of to keep warm. B's studio was all windows and the sun shone in to make it lovely and light.

Bramble was in walking distance of us now. She lived with two other 'orses, Battie, who was 30 years old and would chase dogs (I tried to get 'er to chase me but it never worked!), and Bella, who was soon Bramble's best friend, she was grey and the same age as Bramble.

We were near a lot of other 'ouses so I made lots of new friends. In these 'ouses also lived CATS!!

CATS

The next door neighbour's cats used to climb the fence and come into our garden. This made me cross. Sprout said to bark at them, then they would run. This I tried and would shoot out of B's studio and bark as soon as I saw them. They would leap up over the fence and back to their gardens and I would bark and run round in circles. I learnt that all you 'ad to do was bark at them to make them run, so when walking to Brambles 'ome I would run round the 'ouses looking for cats. Though some were older and wiser and wouldn't run, they would bash me with their paws, OH it did 'urt so!! They were bigger than me.

AROUND SUFFOLK

We enjoyed lots of long walks, and rides on Bramble. It was riding that I saw me first deer. Sprout got very excited and started barking. B urged Bramble into a canter after the deer. I 'ang on for grim death; it was really fun but also scary at the same time!! I was getting so much better at balancing; I did still 'ave me 'arness on just in case.

Clemetis was of course much taller than us so she could see the deer when we were walking. We could smell them but in the tall grass we couldn't see a thing. B would lift us up and we would bark and bark with joy at seeing the deer, then we would be put back down and could see nothing. No fair!!

JAN & JESSIE

Jan was a lovely animal-loving older lady who lived close enough to walk over to. She 'ad a rescued dog called Jessie. Jessie 'ad spent a long time in a dog's 'ome. She didn't like 'unting, but she loved to play ball. We all 'ad loads of toys and balls, so would bring them with us when we visited. Sprout and I loved to play with these toys, but Clemetis thought it a bit below 'er to do so!! Jessie would not do teddies at all, she just stuck to playing ball.

Jan's farm used to have lots of animals on it, so there were lots of buildings to explore. They were full of smells of all sorts of small creatures. We 'ad such fun 'ere. It was a wonderful place to visit.

STAYING WITH MRS SMITH

When B 'ad to go off without us, we would stay at Mrs. Smith's 'ouse. We liked this as there was lots of 'unting to do 'ere. Mrs. Smith would take us in the car to where we would walk a couple of times a day. It was always very noisy in the car with six of us. Clemetis would be 'owling, Pie, Pickle, Sprout and I were barking, of course. Buzzie didn't really join in as he didn't understand all the fuss.

We would arrive at the woods to walk, and pile out the car all still barking, run off and 'unt straight away. There were deer 'ere, they were smaller than ones we'd seen before, but could really run and jump. It was not long before they 'ad got away from us. Mrs. Smith used to get quite cross, as the only one left with 'er was Buzzie. We could 'ear 'er shouting "get back 'ere you DESPICABLE puppies." We 'ad no idea what this meant, but thought it best to go back!!

'UNTING TRIP WITH BEAN

If B was away for any length of time Clemetis used to stay at Mrs Smith's, and Sprout and I used to stay at Kim and Nick's. We did miss Clemetis, but loved staying with Bean and the beagles. There was always lots of 'unting' to do round the buildings.

One day Bean and I were 'unting bunnies and found we 'ad come to a road, we crossed it and carried on, came to another road. We could still smell the bunnies so crossed this one as well. We found an 'edge with loads of 'oles and started to dig and dig.

We were 'aving so much fun we lost track of time. It 'ad gotten dark. Bean says "listen I can 'ear Nick." We ran off in the direction of 'is voice. 'E was pleased to see us. We got into the car, Bean on Nick's knee and me on the seat beside. All at once Nick stopped the car, and looked at Bean's tummy. She did yelp. She 'ad cut 'erself whilst 'unting. We went to the vet's and she 'ad to be stitched up. She was very sore. We were not allowed out together for a long time, YES, I was in TROUBLE again!!

B'S NEW CAR

B came 'ome with a lovely little black shiny car. It 'ad no roof and only two seats. Sprout and I would sit on a small shelf behind B and Clemetis. It made us 'igher up than them. We could see all the animals to 'unt from 'ere, so we barked and whined all the way through the journeys! We loved going to town on shopping trips. Sprout and I were the centers of attention sitting up at the back of the car.

I liked that.

THE BIG BUNNY

The days were taken up with riding, walking and 'unting round the farm where Bramble lived. The fields surrounding the farm 'ad loads of bunnies. I've never caught anything but this did not make me any less enthusiastic. There were also chickens 'ere but I was not to even look at them. Bella's owner 'ad guinea pigs and a bunny, 'e was big with floppy ears. When I barked 'e just looked at me and twitched 'is nose. The guinea pigs squeaked and waddled round their pen. B told me off for barking at them, I did enjoy doing it though. "Be quiet" she shouted. OOOPS in TROUBLE again!!

TOADS

On a rainy day I was looking in one of the ditches filled with water by the side of Bramble's field, I found a strange crawly fing under a rock. I poked it with me nose and it crawled some more, I barked at it and it blinked at me, so I popped it in me mouth and swallowed it. It slid down to me tummy. Me tummy turned inside out!! Me eyes watered, me mouth foamed up. I was so sick, I sicked 'im up and 'e crawled off. It were a toad. YUCK! I kept being sick. I thought I would die. B carried me 'ome. I was bad all day, I don't like toads!!

To cheer me up Sprout brought one of 'er teddies for me to play with. We played tug of war until 'e split. There was fluff everywhere. B got a little cross but not for long.

B GETS STUCK

It was a lovely evening and we 'ad walked over to see Jan and Jessie. As we darted through the gate Clemetis caught site of a big bunny. The 'unt was on. We all chased 'im into a big pile of tin. Clemetis was really barking. I shot round the other side where I could get under the pile and see it. I barked and barked. Sprout flew in behind me. Unfortunately Sprout is a little rounder than me and got stuck fast in the 'ole behind me. B, Jessie and Jan came to see what was going on. Realizing what 'ad 'appened, B started moving the tin. Out shot the bunny, with Clemetis right on it's bob tail, but Sprout and I were still stuck. She 'ad blocked me exit.

B got us out and off we shot, in our 'urry we 'ad toppled the tin and it fell right on top of B. Clemetis worried about the commotion, rushed back only to jump on top of the tin that was on top of B. "Get off, get off" cried B. Clemetis was very confused but being so well be'aved did as she was told. B was wedged under the tin now. All you could see were 'er 'ead and shoulders.She wiggled and wiggled and eventually got out. We never did catch that bunny!!!

SPROUT AND THE 'OLE

On a sunny 'ot morning Sprout decided she was going to 'unt for frogs. B and Clemetis were brushing Bramble off after our ride. There were a ditch beside the stables that 'ad some water in it. Sprout sat in the water to cool off before setting about the frogs. I was 'unting up and down the banks. Sprout announced she were ready now so off she went slowly along the water, nose down, trying to find the scent. I decided against the frogs, after me t'do with the toad, and went to the 'ay barn to 'unt mice. No sooner than I were on the scent than B calls out to us saying she's on the way 'ome.

I reluctantly gave up the chase and went to B. Clemetis were there with 'er but there were no sign of Sprout. B called and called. We were all getting very worried. This were not like Sprout, she always came when called. We all went to the ditch and started looking up and down. Suddenly B said she could 'ear something. Running into the ditch were clay drain pipes from the fields. B rushed to one of them and listened. There was a definite clinking noise. Some bubbles started to appear in the water coming out of it. All at once like a cork from a bottle out shot a very wet and dirty Sprout, SPLASH, straight into the water. Sprout was rather embarrassed by the 'ole ordeal, but we were just glad to see 'er.

GOING TO AMERICA

It wasn't long after Sprout's ordeal that B was packing the Land Rover again. This time she also added three large boxes. These were our travel boxes, as we were all going to America. Clemetis said "we don't drive all the way!" Sprout and Clemetis 'ad both lived there with B and Bramble before.

I liked that.

BELINDA SILLARS grew up in rural Suffolk, surrounded by many different animals. She became a professional artist and sculptor in her twenties, and her work became very popular and sold widely. She now works primarily for private commission. In early 2000 she moved to Virginia, and now splits her time between England and the United States. Her family of animals accompanies her wherever she goes and provides her continual inspiration.